SOUND GUARDIANS
INTERCEDING
MINSTRELS

Sound Guardians Interceding Minstrels

Myra L Johnson

Dedication

This book is dedicated to my Mother R. M. Johnson for allowing me to explore my passion for music. Her love and support encouraged me to step out to break barriers as a young lady that played drums.

To the Late Pastor Brenda Jefferson my first Minister of Music that took time to mentor, instruct, and teach" GOD is not hard up to accept any old type of praise." Her genuine care about Minstrels holistic well-being with discipline concerning service to GOD has shaped how I operate as a Minstrel. Your legacy will continue.

To Mr. Kenny Cornish My drumming instructor that instilled" playing with a group for the music and not for self".

To all my Musician Family of Church "Uncles, Cousins, Brothers, Nephews, Nieces, and Sisters "the sharpening of my gift through our serving together has pushed me to grow and find the Sound.

Contents

INTRODUCTION

BOOM!!! BANG!!! CRASH!! BAM!! POP POP, POP!! "Conjunction Junction what's your function" Now that I have your attention. How many were looking for the description for the sound effects? How many sang the rest of the song? (If you know that song you are of a certain age. No judgement I'm just saying.) We are bombarded by sound. Everyday all day. It can and has conditioned us.

Sound is being used in a plethora of ways. Current culture is adamant concerning opening up higher states of consciousness through frequency, and vibration. People seek out drum meditation. Subjecting themselves to gong washing and frequency healing. Grand quantities of people have chanted "ohm" in hopes to find their resonant frequency to achieve inner peace. Many are drawn to drum circles to "interface with a higher power".

Some seek solace in the absence of sound completely   through sensory deprivation in hopes of opening up hidden pathways to enlightening energy.

Introduction

Sound is being appropriated. Djembe drums are played all over the world. Descendants of those who once opposed, suppressed and outlawed, even persecuted the practice of Africans drumming. Now are leading drum circles and giving TEDx talks on the efficacy of the practice. Suburban sports teams perform South Pacific Haka in hopes that the vibration gives them the edge. Secular music has sought to know the "secret sauce" of Gospel drumming. Seeking that same energy and sound by employing the Player. Sometimes taking whole bands. Scouting and recruiting Musicians like the athletic drafts.

We have been trained. The sound of a bell could mean wake up, time for class, lunch break is over. We ring the bell for service at small businesses or the dinner bell for food. "Apostle J. McCaa 100 Days of Praise 2/25/2024; talked of the bells of a clock heard throughout a town to let you know what time it is...." He went on to discuss that the bells were normally in the churches. We as the Kingdom of God should influence the times and seasons "This also applies to the sound released into the Earth. Culture illegally wants these experiences and high feelings, opening doors to energies, frequencies, vibrations, secret sauce void of the Main ingredient GOD. We within the kingdom of GOD are to set the tone. Culture desires the euphoria outside and void of GOD. It also desires to take God given sound and pervert it.

We as Musicians of the Most High God are called to intercede. Our Worship and adoration of GOD becomes a technology to direct people to the way which is JESUS – the Way the truth and the life. This is the enlightenment that is needed not just to bring a temporary interface but an encounter that leads to engaging with God.

1

What Is Sound?

Let us understand what is Sound? Simply Sound is -What you hear. It is not always perceived through the ears. Sound is made of vibration, frequency, and concussion. We may have heard before" If a tree falls in the woods and no one was there did it make a sound?" My answer is yes! We may not have been there; however, the tree struck the earth as an incredibly huge drumstick to a greater sized drum. There was percussion and concussion. People who have diminished hearing can still perceive sound. We feel sound. Dancers feel the music with their feet and their ears. We can feel the vibration of sound from traffic. A semi-truck hits uneven pavement or a maintenance hole cover in a lane opposing your vehicle everything shakes. Sound invades. It can infect, affect, and effect even affect infest. Sound has overtaking power. Hostile situations we have witnessed the use of the flash grenades that smoke and produce a sound that throws off the equilibrium of all nearby. Walking in a grocery store minding your own business, the music is playing as you look for Tarragon. Before you are aware the song playing has infected you. You are now humming or singing lyrics you really care nothing for. Even worse you cannot seem to let the melody loose from your mind. You have been

1

infested with "Grocery Store FM "and may or may not have found the Tarragon.

Sound is defined as "Vibrations that travel through air or another medium and can be heard when they reach a person's or animal's ear, produced by regular and continuous vibrations as opposed to noise." (Oxford Language Dictionary) "A vibration of air caused by a collision of bodies or other means, sufficient to affect the auditory nerves when perfect. To make an impulse of the air that shall strike the organs of hearing with a particular effect." (Noah Webster 1828 Dictionary) "Sound is a vibration that propagates as an acoustic wave through a transmission medium such as gas, liquid or solid. In human physiology and psychology sound is the reception of such waves and their perceptions by the Brian" (Wikapedia)

Noise according to Noah Webster 1828 "Is a sound of any kind proceeding from any cause, outcry, clamor to sound loud". According to Oxford Language Dictionary "A sound especially loud or unpleasant that causes disturbance." Wikapedia states " unwanted or harmful sound considered unpleasant , loud or disruptive to hearing" It also goes on to state that they are from a physics stand point there is no distinction between noise and desired sound as both are vibrations through a medium… the difference arises when the Brian receives and perceives a sound." So, noise can be considered the unwanted part of sound or tainted sound. An example of this: in music situation feedback from a microphone or plugging something into an unshielded outlet and it buzzes. It is interference of the pure sound.

Another component of sound is Vibration: a trembling motion. According to Merrium-Webster "a rapid motion of an elastic body or substance back and forth." Oxford states Percussion the striking of a solid object with or against another with some degree of force" Concussion: A violent shock from a heavy blow" Then the other component is Frequency: the rate in which something occurs. The faster the vibration the higher the frequency.

Sound: founded in truth, firm, solid, valid, cannot be refuted or overthrown. Right, correct, free from error. It can also be described as: laid on with force This definition from Noah Webster 1828

Now that we have defined sound and noise let us dive slightly deeper into the matter.

This world was activated by sound. "Then GOD said 'LET THER BE LIGHT!! (Most of us tend to read this and think of GOD's voice being loud and Monstrous. Just an observation.) HE called the light Day the darkness Night. Then GOD said "Let there be a firmament in the middle of the waters, let it divide the waters from the waters. He called the firmament heaven. He said Let the waters under heavens be gathered together in to one place and let the dry land appear and it was so. Genesis Chapters 1&2 account of the Earth's origin. John 1:1-3 In the beginning was the Word and the Word was with GOD and the WORD was GOD He was in the beginning with GOD. Revelation 1:15b His voice as the sound of many waters. KJV Bible

We see the creative powers of sound. How GOD'S voice is described as sounding like many waters. Let that evoke sounds of Niagara Falls, level ten rapids, the crashing of Fifty story waves in the ocean. The Ruach wind of GOD moving in these instances to create the outcomes dictated. ABBA infected the atmosphere with HIS sound. HE laid on with force. This affected the void and formlessness of the Earth causing the effect of light and darkness. The infestation of Jehovah's sound caused life to come in the waters and on the land. ABBA" breathed into Man and he became a living soul." We were infested with the breath of GOD. The sound of GOD's breath is in us!!!

Pause and reflect on that! -Selah! Knowing now that Sound is capable of infecting, affecting, effecting, and infesting, we must make sure that the Sound released is Sound. Pure not distorted with unwanted pollutants. Pollutants of Secular appropriation, taking the sounds and those skilled to produce sound sanctioned to lead us to the throne of GOD and detouring us to Idols. Culture wants access to Godly things without relationship with GOD. They want the feeling of euphoria with all the altered states of false consciousness. They attend a gong washing or drum circle. Thinking they have interfaced with a "higher power" without the revelation of repentance and relationship. Sound: founded in truth- John 14:6 JESUS says, "I am the way the truth and the life no man comes to the Father except by ME." NKJV

We as believers are called to pray and intercede- stand in the gap. Intercessors are called to guard-Shamar specific areas. Minstrels are given charge over sound. We are responsible for the sound sanctioned to lead to God. We are SOUND GUARDIANS!

2

Origin of Sound

Now that we know what components make up Sound. Let us trace its origin. According to Genesis 4:19-21 the first mention of sound as music comes with Lamech's son Jubal (Cain's Fourth great grandson) 'He was the Father of all those who play the harp and flute." Jubal – Stream or Ram's horn.

The second mention of Music is in Exodus 15: 1-21 After the Lord rescued Israel from Egypt. The Songs of Moses and Miriam. Miriam the Prophetess and the women took up Timbrel and Dance This Song was of what and how GOD rescued them, GOD in HIS power and greatness. Prior to the songs imagine the sound of the East wind that came to cut a path in the Red Sea. That wind dried the land on the path for them to cross and for chariot wheels to roll. (They still find remnants of chariot wheels gilded in gold.)

Leviticus 19 Speaks of the sound of thunder and the trumpet getting louder as Moses was summoned to the Mt. Sinai to meet with God. Numbers 10 speaks concerning two silver trumpets being fashioned to give directions as to how the Camp moves. Whether to the next location or just to gather to hear instruction.

Numbers 10:8-10 The Sons of Aaron, the priests shall blow the trumpets; and these shall be to you as an ordinance forever throughout your generations.". when you go to war in your land against an enemy that oppresses you... sound an alarm with the trumpets and you will be remembered before the LORD your GOD and you will be saved from your enemies." Also, in the day of your gladness, appointed feasts, beginning of the months, you shall blow the trumpet...burnt offerings and sacrifices of peace offerings they shall be a memorial for you before your GOD. I am the LORD your GOD. Trumpets were used in war Numbers 31: 8" ... Eleazer the priest with the holy articles and signal trumpets in His hand".

When the Children of Israel from occupation to overtaking Jerico the sound of the trumpets blew the whole duration. Also, in the book of Joshua 10 sounds of large hailstones "that the LORD cast down from heaven" ... God got in the fight. Later in verse 12-14 Joshua commands" the sun and moon to stand still". Joshua used his GOD given authority to complete the GOD assigned task.

The Children of Israel sung a song concerning water in the desert Numbers 21: 16-18. God opened the mouth of a Balaam's Donkey to speak words he understood. Numbers 22:22-33 Moses sang over the children of Israel after rehearsing the Laws of God the blessings and cursing to remind them of who they were and who GOD is to them. Duet.32 2-43. A reminder with music.

Judges 5 gives us the victory song of Deborah Judge of Israel. Judges 6 Gideon calls for back up with the trumpet. Judges chapter 7 Gideon/ Jerubbaal arms Three hundred men with pitchers, lamps and trumpets against an opponent that had numerous camels and people. Gideon and company described it as' a loaf of barley bread tumbling in the midst, destroying a tent" Not only a tent but the opponent turned against itself. The sound of breaking pitchers and the trumpets with the chant "The sword of the LORD and of Gideon !!!" caused calamity. They did not use their weapons.

1 Samuel 10 during the anointing process of Saul he was sent to encounter the prophets coming off the hill of the LORD with stringed instruments, flute, tambourine, harp, the prophetic music caused Saul to prophesy. Chapter 12 of1 Samuel verses 13 -25. Israel is being reminded of the poor choices being made, Samuel calls thunder and rain, the people are frightened, Samuel urges them to do the good they have been taught. Expressing his displeasure but not relinquishing his post as intercessor.

Samuel did this again as Saul was rejected by the Lord 1Samuel 15 He reminded Saul of the oath he took and the transgression he made. Samuel rebuked Saul. Then stated GOD had demoted him. Samuell grieved for Saul. Saul knew better. Not only did this grieve Samuel it grieved GOD also.

David is anointed 1Sam 16:13 Later in the same chapter David is called to minister on his harp for Saul several times. Observation: The disturbing spirit of Saul came from the LORD. Saul's first encounter after being anointed was with the minstrel/prophets coming from the meeting place with God. Now for Saul to hear David play taking him back to his first encounter with God. Wow Then Saul's awareness that God will not allow him to ascend to his former relationship status with God. Now only a shadow of it through David's playing. Each time being reminded that you have been demoted.

When it gets to Chapter 18 after David has defeated Goliath, the song that the Women sang and played (Yes as a women Minstrel/Musician this needed to be highlighted.) for David 1 Samuel 18:5-9 Gave Saul the narrow eye toward David. This song lasted well into 2 Samuel   However David loved Saul. When the death of Saul and Jonathon occurred, David wrote "The Song of the Bow" 2 Samuel 1. He wrote a song of Mourning for Abner 2 SAM 3:34 There were sounds of mourning, weeping, and travailing. The sound and action of Worship 2 Sam 6 5 "...David and all the House of Israel played on all kinds of instruments made of Fir...harps, psaltery, on timbrels, cornets, and cymbals. Later in the same chapter vs 13,14,15 The Ark went six places they stopped and offered oxen and fatlings, David wearing a linen Ephod danced before the LORD with all his might, they brought up the ARK with the sound of shouting and the trumpet. "They also went home with food. Vs 19 A cake of bread, a skin of wine and a piece of meat. 1 Chronicles 15: 25 David organizes the Levites, the musicians/ Minstrels. They were singers that played instruments, they taught and were psalmists and prophetic. The ARK of the covenant was accompanied by Priests with trumpets. There is a sound that accompanies the presence of God.

1 Kings 17 Elijah the Tishbite and Prophet, then Elisha the student use sound to judge a region. He spoke what GOD was saying to his region   withheld the rain on His word. The Sound activation, we speak what GOD says, and the demonstration follows. This follows throughout the Old Testament. The declaration of what GOD was going to do was announced. Conditions of obedience and compliance were necessary to avoid these outcomes. However, the hardhearted and stiff-necked posture of the people caused all that was declared would in fact be demonstrated. The perversion of sound in Daniel Chapter 3 :4 "... O peoples, nations, and languages when you hear the horn, flute, lyre, and psaltery in symphony with all types of music you shall fall down and worship the golden image... Whoever does not. will be cast into burning fiery furnace." A National decree for

idolatry using music. Sounds of a roaring furnace in Daniel that consumed the men that put the three Hebrew Boys into it. Further in the book of Daniel (4) "A voice fell from heaven". This voice spoke of the demise of the King at his own pride.

The New Testament we see the sound of John the Baptist preparing for the way of the LORD- WORD (JESUS). We also hear the voice from heaven "This is My beloved Son in whom I am well pleased." We hear the words of JESUS shape us into the image of the Father. His voice teaches us how to use our authority as Sons, Priests, and Kings of the Most High. His voice demonstrates how we overthrow the temptation of Satan "it is written"- we take the proper legal action.

3

Appropriations

ppropriation- the act of taking something for one's own use typically without the owner's permission. This is according to Oxford Dictionary. To expand on this definition, to acquire something of another person treat it as your own without acknowledgement. This can also describe a financial action: A sum of money or total of assets devoted to a certain purpose. (Oxford Dictionary).

Let us also explore Cultural appropriations: the unacknowledged or inappropriate adoptions of the customs, practices etc. of one people or society by members of another and typically more dominant people or society. (Oxford Dictionary). We have established appropriating is a form of taking without asking or acknowledging the people or entity it came from. Pilfering, cuffing, boosting, lifting, plagiarizing, all of this.

The mismanagement of another society's culture; the art, fashion, food, music, amusement, Spiritual Beliefs, colloquialisms by the mainstream for their amusement, monetary and social gain without acknowledgement, reparations, or apology.

Reflecting on the introduction. suburban soccer teams perform Haka in their warmups. Hoping this Maori war dance will give them the edge. They may have seen it or heard it and thought it would be a nice exotic entertainment before the game. These teams have no connection to the culture or culture it originates from.

African / African American culture has been pilfered without recognition. Adopted then adapted – perverted it from its original intent.

The Djembe drum originating in the Mali empire is played from West Africa to South Africa. The drum and accompanying instruments and those that play them have a place of honor. The artisans have a place of honor. They select a log of specific woods Lenke, Hare,' Iroko, Guile' cut it carve it, sand it smooth by hand. They place carvings of significance on the side. The drum hides a goat that was eaten or a cow. This drum was never to be struck with a stick nor to be put on the ground unless being repaired or attached to a drummer in the dance. Djembe is known as the healing drum. Used for military, music, community and religion, this drum was a way of communication.

Now this drum is played by descendants of those who enslaved and forbade Africans drumming. Those that love drums have started drumming circles with the Djembe as if it were theirs and their culture. Many celebrations the djembe is present, being struck by drumsticks or with bass drum beaters. When you take something outside of its purpose it is abuse. Sometimes it is difficult to find authentic djembes and those who teach, not just rhythms but the culture and specific significance and language that accompanies the drum. There are drums made in Indonesia, Thailand that claim to be djembes. Wood workers in the USA that make drums of Black walnut or Elm, turn the wood on machines- not authentic. African American songs, colloquialisms, fashion, inventions, and contribution have been stolen and monetized by those outside the African American community. These examples show how subtle and overt appropriation can be. How appropriation from those that have no connection, or investment can dilute the intended outcomes.

Likewise, when sound that is intended for worship unto the Most High GOD is taken out of context by those that have no desire to know GOD but want the euphoria, heighten senses of awareness doors have been opened for disrespect and idolatry.

Moses is summoned to the mountain to meet with God in Exodus 19, returning in Exodus 32 he hears a sound of perverted celebration around an Idol. The people got impatient saying" we do not know what has become of Moses." Earlier in the book of Exodus 19 the people were afraid of GOD because of the sounds coming from the mountain. These same people had the gumption to want to create an idol god and a sound associated with it for worship. When they had previously been instructed how to purify themselves to Worship the Almighty God. Right here they disrespected GOD with the Sound of perversion chasing an idol.

I also stated earlier how appropriation is a form of abuse through misuse Leviticus 10 the sons of Aaron offered to GOD strange fire. There was a particular way incense was to be presented to the Lord of Hosts. They had been trained the proper way. They imitated what and how this was to be facilitated.

When the imitation of a sound or process dedicated and called HOLY is mocked there are repercussions. Levitus 10;2,3 speaks of fire coming from the Lord incinerating Aaron's sons for offering" Strange fire before the Lord" God's response "by those who come near me I must be regarded as Holy and before all the people I must be glorified."

King Nebuchadnezzar of Babylon in the Book of Daniel had a National mandate for Sound to be used as command to worship an Idol. Punishment for disobedience was placement in a furnace with a temperature exceeding seven times its normal. The Hebrew boys did not worship the idol, they worshipped GOD. Subsequently being questioned and threatened with death. While being thrown into the furnace, the attendants throwing was consumed by the fire. The Hebrews were found in the fire walking freely completely unscathed. Changing the heart of the King to say Jehovah is God. Declaring no one disrespect this God. King Nebuchadnezzar after this occurrence was lifted in pride and arrogance which caused him to disrespect God. Resulting in a seven-year state of insanity involving the King to act as an animal.

King Belshazzar of Babylon son of Nebuchadnezzar in the book of Daniel took the consecrated articles dedicated for worship from the house of GOD to have a drinking party. One would reason that after The Almighty GOD showed Himself through the fiery furnace, A voice from heaven, prior to his Father's pride reducing him to animal behavior, which disrespecting the Almighty GOD would not be wise. Yet Belshazzar drank wine from the sacred articles from the house of GOD. Prompting the writing on the wall by a hand without a body from the LORD, stating the Kingdom would be taken from Belshazzar. That same night the King was murdered, fulfilling what was written on the wall.

When we seek a good better than GOD we are entering into idolatry. When we look for pathways to Godly things, power, presence, knowledge, wisdom, understanding yet no desire to acknowledge or engage fully with GOD we walk in disrespect.

We as Sound Guardians must ensure that we do not allow cultural or national mandates to pollute nor steal neither disrespect the Holiness of God. We should not allow the holy sounds of worship to GOD be perverted into idolatry.

4

Who Is a Minstrel?

We have heard this term or description what does it mean? "A Minstrel: Highly skilled in playing instruments. What sets them apart from just being a musician is that they are specifically anointed to hear and play sounds directly from Heaven. Minstrels invoke the presence of the Highest God through melodies, harmonies, and rhythms that they play..." (-Tabitha Y. Hougabook the Minstrel Speaks.) What is our function?

Primarily we need an intimate relationship with God to know what he desires us to release through our instruments. "Being a Minstrel is more than being talented or gifted. Gifts come without repentance Rom.11:29 Being a Minstrel requires a surrendered heart and spirit... (The Minstrel Speaks) We must be submitted to Holy Spirit to know what is needed in ministry and deliverance."

Dictionary.com states Minstrel a medieval wandering musician who performed songs or recited poetry with instrumental accompaniment. We spoke of appropriation being a form of disrespect, perversion. Another definition of Minstrel is a white actor wearing blackface to do degrading representations of African Americans. So distant from the original intent.

1 Chronicles 25:1-6 speaks of the assigned areas of the minstrels David appointed. These minstrels were highly skilled and the level of consecration to GOD allowed them to prophesy and see through HOLY SPIRIT.

We as Minstrels are priests dedicated and consecrated to the MOST HIGH GOD. We have a relationship with the Father. Spending time in HIS presence to know what HE likes and what displeases HIM. What frequencies, melodies, progressions, vibrations, and rhythms are to be released. Minstrels stand as gatekeepers, doorways, conduits to the sound of the LORD. An unshielded wire picks up interference or distortion producing dirty power releasing a polluted sound. We shield and ground our life and sound with HOLY SPIRIT and the Word of GOD to produce the sound of GOD's Kingdom.

A Musician can play their instrument, sound great be pleasing to the ears making your toes tap giving all the "feels." When a Minstrel releases their sound an encounter with GOD occurs. The sound released is not in competition with anyone it does not have to nor is there a need for it. We being infested with the breath of both the Pneuma and Ruach of the Lord and our playing is an extension of the intimacy. Our playing becomes a living organism. Ushering people to revelation of HIM and relationship with CHRIST.

This is the "Secret sauce" the world is chasing. They desire the encounter with the sound or the feel with out the breath or relationship with GOD. So, they hum and chant "Ohm" for hours trying to find the euphoria. An ohm is a unit of impedance or resistance an obstacle- something in the path. Chanting an obstacle just clutters the way. Gong washing- when a gong is struck forcefully, and the wave of vibration comes or washes over the person. This feels good, it tickles the ear, excites the senses. What was the announcement made by striking the gong? What entered or left the space? What encounter occurred by participating in this activity? Restating the world wants creation without the CREATOR. We as Minstrels stand as gatekeepers and watchmen. A Minstrel is a praying, interceding Priest with an instrument, that also instructs.

5

How We Guard

Minstrels we guard these sacred places of sound by knowing our Identity and assignment. Our relationship with ELOHIM must be constantly cultivated. Priests minister to the LORD, then are an intermediary between GOD and the people. We bring the sounds from the Kingdom of God to the Earth. We Shamar the selah moments. Unlike the sensory deprivation chamber where one's own heartbeat and respiration are mistaken for enlightenment. Selah moments – when we quietly think about how GOD has made HIS presence known.

We must stand steadfast as priests not wavering as Aaron did in Exodus 32. He made the golden calf because he feared the people. He provided the means for idolatry. He opened the gate. No compromising the standard of the MOST HIGH.

1 Chronicles 25

New King James Version

The Musicians

25 Moreover David and the captains of the army separated for the service *some* of the sons of Asaph, of Heman, and of Jeduthun, who *should* prophesy with harps, stringed instruments, and cymbals. And the number of the skilled men performing their

service was: [2]Of the sons of Asaph: Zaccur, Joseph, Nethaniah, and [a]Asharelah; the sons of Asaph were [b]under the direction of Asaph, who prophesied according to the order of the king. [3]Of Jeduthun, the sons of Jeduthun: Gedaliah, [c]Zeri, Jeshaiah, [d]*Shimei*, Hashabiah, and Mattithiah, [e]six, under the direction of their father Jeduthun, who prophesied with a harp to give thanks and to praise the Lord. [4]Of Heman, the sons of Heman: Bukkiah, Mattaniah, [f]Uzziel, [g]Shebuel, [h]Jerimoth, Hananiah, Hanani, Eliathah, Giddalti, Romamti-Ezer, Joshbekashah, Mallothi, Hothir, *and* Mahazioth. [5]All these *were* the sons of Heman the king's seer in the words of God, to [i]exalt his horn. For God gave Heman fourteen sons and three daughters.

[6]All these *were* under the direction of their father for the music *in* the house of the Lord, with cymbals, stringed instruments, and harps, for the service of the house of God. Asaph, Jeduthun, and Heman *were* under the authority of the king. [7]So the number of them, with their brethren who were instructed in the songs of the Lord, all who were skillful, *was* two hundred and eighty-eight.

Now we see that Asaph, Heman and Jeduthan were set over those who prophesied with instruments. These men were captains in David's army. They had a strategy to defeat an enemy. We as intercessors have this same character to defeat our adversary the devil.

Each of the three men and their families were responsible for an area to cover by playing music. Asaph prophesied according to the King's order. He had to be close to the King to know His orders. Likewise, we need to have that relationship with JESUS our King to know His orders. Jeduthun prophesied with a harp to give thanks and praise to the LORD. Jeduthun was the creative, breaking out with fresh praise after decrees and announcements from on HIGH. Our praise and thanksgiving should never be canned or stagnant. We always have new praise and adoration for our GOD. Heman was a seer so he played his horn and his sons and daughters to announce what is coming. We use our music to announce what GOD says is to come. Our worship and consecration to GOD with dedication to releasing Holy sound from GOD'S heart makes us Minstrels. Protecting the way and instructing those to come after us is how we become SOUND GUADIANS.

Before I started playing music, I asked God to allow me to praise Him on any instrument He would bless me to encounter. I loved JESUS and was young and shy, so music became my voice, my therapy, my meeting place with the Lord. I would save lunch money to invest in drumsticks. I prayed and fasted, studied the Word of God. I wanted to know God. My Music Pastor Brenda Jefferson placed me in environments to learn how to discern the move of GOD and to stay humble. Years later the LORD allowed my gifts to make room for me. My heart posture toward Elohim matters. There was a time where my heart was hurt, from life, people, and circumstances. I sat myself down. I acknowledged that I was disconnected. What I would release by an instrument would also be disconnected and polluted. I did not and would not play my drum set, only practicing rudiments on a cushion. My conga drums became decorated, large clothing racks. I had a fear of touching my djembe drum (even to move it about in my space in its case) apprehensive of what might manifest. Knowing that drum holds a special spiritual gravity. The awareness that I am a gate a door and conduit plus my love for JESUS would not allow any release of sound. I did not want to play my issues on to the people. When I allowed HOLY SPIRIT to heal me, having deep encounter with HIM. Allowing HOLY SPIRIT into those places others were not permitted, was the key to getting our relationship repaired. This equipped me to return to playing.

I witnessed something at a drum circle. This was a community event sponsored by a local music store. I was invited ("volun-told") by my Djembe/conga instructor to attend. So, I and two others from the drumming village were there. An Elder drummer well-seasoned in years and hands (all congas all the time) that also helped with our instruction. My Cousin was also there. We both played for a local dance troupe. We are there to assist our Big Brother G. who is facilitating with a broken finger in a splint. There are at least thirty people there. They came with a menagerie of items: mechanical djembes, bongos, frame drums, even a washboard and spoons. There was an air of pride and slight appropriation in the circle concerning their adeptness.

The rhythm started Bro. G. told them when he points to them to solo over the music. Bro. Elder was irritated at the attitude of the people and said" Music is a language. I f you have nothing to say please do not play" His face said more than his words. The Rhythm is up and moving Bro. G. points to different ones for solos, Cousin and I take solos. Now Bro. Elder takes a solo. My Cousin and I thought we were hearing things. Bro. Elder began his solo, never saying a word. His drumming and drums began to sound like words to us. He cussed and cursed the people out with his hands. When the solo heated up so did the level of cussing with his hands. His solo sounded great the people came and gave kudos to Bro Elder not knowing the fullness of the infection. What did he release? Curses and the people did not know, accepting with applause.

I prayed "Jesus this man just cussed all the people out with his hands not opening his mouth. Father allows me to heal people when I play. Let your fragrance of Your presence be released in Jesus Name."

Take time to evaluate your stance as one who plays an instrument. Ask GOD to give you a clean heart and hands to stand before HIM and his people to release the sound of HIS heart. Pray that your sound ushers people into encounter with Jesus and not just vibe to the groove. Let us stand in the gateways as Guardians and not a revolving door for Idolatry. Let us love GOD more than all the world can offer. May the love and sound of the LORD permeate your hearts in the Name of JESUS.

Myra Johnson is an Illinois native, Business Owner, Minstrel, and a Creative. She has a passion for pursuing GOD's heart through worship and intercession. Myra is a licensed and ordained Elder and a Drummer/Percussionist.. Her love for GOD is demonstrated by decades of service in Music Ministry.

www.ingramcontent.com/pod-product-compliance
Lightning Source LLC
Chambersburg PA
CBHW061648130726
47996CB00003B/1503